WHAT PEOPLE ARE SAYING ABOUT
REAL PEOPLE, REAL WORK

"Real People, Real Work gave our management team **a starting place to talk about the REAL issues facing our service business**—and once we did that, we were able to solve them. When people read these simple stories —**the light bulb goes on**—and for the first time **they understand the impact of customer perception and process improvement on the bottom line."**

Norena Gutierrez, Quality Manager, Hewlett-Packard Company

"An engaging series of stories and anecdotes about Quality in Everyday Life. **A non-statistical, easy-reading book** that sets the stage for Quality Improvement Programs."

Dan Seymour, Author of *On Q: Causing Quality in Higher Education*

"Real People, Real Work is a **thought-provoking book for** *managers* thinking about how to be *leaders*. It would also be a nice augmentation for "how-to" materials."

Dr. Andrew C. Palm, Director of Statistical Methods
James River Corporation

"If you own a business, if you manage part of a business, or if you work for a business, **you ought to read this book."**

Timothy Fuller, Quality Consultant, Fuller Associates

"The world would be a better place if more people would read this book."

Michael Hernke, Student, University of Wisconsin

"It's the simple things in life that are really profound."

Chet Harmer, Director of Quality Training, Coopers and Lybrand

"I don't know if the book is a primer or advanced text. It may be both."

David Couper, Police Chief: Madison, Wisconsin

"I loved it!" (Consistent comment from readers everywhere.)

REAL PEOPLE
REAL WORK

Parables on Leadership in the 90's

Lee Cheaney

Maury Cotter

SPC Press, Inc.
Knoxville, Tennessee

Editor
Warren Gaskill

Technical Editor for SPC Press
David J. Wheeler

ISBN 0-945320-11-6   123456789

This book is dedicated to
the guy in the box in the lobby.

And to "The Golden Eagles."

And to all the other real people
who lived these stories.

CONTENTS

SETTING THE STAGE

THE STORIES

One

Two

Three

Four

Five

DISCUSSION STARTERS

FOREWORD BY
PETER SCHOLTES

In the Quality Movement we emphasize that work is done through systems, processes, and methods. We preach the importance of monitoring the key indicators and recording the variation in the process. We use flow charts, control charts, the seven basic tools, the seven management tools—all good stuff—very important and very cerebral.

Lee Cheaney and Maury Cotter, of course, know the value of a systems perspective and statistical thinking. But in this collection of anecdotes, they remind us of the abiding reality of our factories and offices: real work is done by real people. The person at the word processor or with the wrench or driving the fork lift has a name and a family, and hopes, fears, insights, and pride. These are the people in the trenches who must work within what one of my clients describes as "*common cause stupidity*," factors beyond their control and that undermine their good efforts. Lee and Maury tell us of everyday frustration, pride, caring, and ingenuity.

The subtitle of this work is "Parables on Leadership." Like classic parables, these contain lessons that are mostly left to the reader to draw out and make explicit. We learn from stories—the oldest, perhaps the most reliable, and certainly the most entertaining way to learn. The leadership of Quality is like unto the guy in the box in the lobby, or a meat inspector alone and under pressure, or a run in your pantyhose (okay, so these aren't exactly Sufi Tales or the Gospel according to Matthew).

There's an old adage that says, "When the student is ready, the teacher will appear." Stories let you draw your own lessons; the ones you are ready to learn. This book can be a rich resource for all of us who are ready to learn everyday lessons from everyday people.

I have some suggestions about this book for leaders, or those who would be leaders:

* Read this book from cover to cover. It's a great airport book, easy to read with short segments.

* When you've finished each story, jot down the points about leadership you got from that story.

*   When you've finished the whole book, look at all the points you've listed. What do they collectively tell you? What were you ready to learn?

*   Which stories stand out for you? Revisit each and try to understand more about why you were touched by it. You may learn not only about leadership, but about yourself.

Peter Scholtes
Madison, Wisconsin
10 September 1990

ACKNOWLEDGEMENTS

Teamwork is one of the key elements of Quality. Without it, this book would be two piles of messy drafts, one in Wisconsin and one in California. Those who played key roles in making it a real book include:

Connie Hall and Jim Gentry, who, on their own initiative, took the drafts and used their graphic design and marketing talents to create the first edition in 1990.

Warren Gaskill, whose sensitive but wise editing strengthened the messages. And whose persistence and dedication to purpose led to this edition and a broader audience.

John Cotter, for forever believing it would happen and for continuous help and support. Kelly and Adam Cotter for their fresh eyes and young wisdom.

SPC Press, for challenging the paradigms about publishing companies and for being a "win-win" organization.

Joiner Associates, the big name company with real people; Nick Kaufman for advising on the development, marketing, and final location of a publisher; and Peter Scholtes for his insightful foreword and creative advice.

Our hundreds of network friends and families, who championed the book, experimented with it, and passed it on.

David Wheeler, whose technical editing at SPC Press hastened the publication of this second edition.

One of the most rewarding parts of working in the Quality field is getting to work with people who have a strong sense of purpose and teamwork. People who believe that a gain is a gain for the whole, and who contribute with their spirits. We feel privileged and honored to be working among these folks.

We hope this book succeeds as a contribution to the vision we share.

SETTING THE STAGE

INTRODUCTION BY MAURY COTTER

The first time I saw Lee Cheaney speak was at a conference on quality in 1987 in Madison, Wisconsin. It was a national conference, featuring the best and the brightest—Great Names from the roots of the movement. They spoke of great new ideas and theories to a crowd of over 500 people who paid $400 each to attend.

I listened to speakers cover the theories with graphs, charts, and lots of numbers. It seemed to make sense. It rang true and blended well with what I thought I believed and what I thought I was doing. But was I? What did the theories really mean?

Between the big sessions in the big room with the big names were some little workshops in little rooms with up-and-coming names. Lee Cheaney was one of those—a small room. The chairs filled up fast. I got a good seat. I had heard he was good.

And he was. He put energy and enthusiasm into his talk. But most of all, he put people into it. He told us about theories and new ideas, but each one was painted with color and real life characters. He told us about Sara who kept a record book for almost ten years—full of columns and numbers, carefully logged and verified—that no one ever looked at. He told us how everyone thought the staff in word processing was slow and lazy, until they worked together and found ways to reduce turn-around from 21 days to eight hours. And he told us about a team of people who didn't know they could be a team, who came together and reduced the number of charge-out cards in their *nine miles of files* from 36 different cards to two.

Cheaney made the connection between theory and real people. His heart and soul were in it.

Over the next two years, I listened to him speak several more times. And, as luck and fate would have it, our paths merged and I found myself working with him, giving a workshop on teamwork in the fall of 1989 in Fond du lac, Wisconsin. He was also giving the closing speech for the conference, his last in state government before he left for a job with industry in California.

It was then, listening to him again, that I realized the significance of those stories. It was the stories that made the light bulb turn on for people. They gave the regular person an idea of how to go back and do it.

And then I thought about the literature on management theory. And how those thick books with little type and big, complex theories are so foreboding to the average person. I graduated from college with honors, and I am bored to death and lost with most of those books. And most people who are leaders of other people are probably even less inclined to read those books. At 6:14 A.M., the light flashed on for me!—I remember it that well. We needed to *write* those stories. Not just tell them in speeches and in training seminars, but write them in a book.

I spilled my idea to Cheaney on a walk that morning, on the way to see a pink house in Fond du lac, and the idea started to take shape. We began working on it that day, and continued, with calls and mail across the continent, to produce this, our first book.

About two months into the writing process, I learned more about why the stories worked. George Box, of the Center for Quality and Productivity Improvement at the University of Wisconsin, talked about *learning frontwards*. He gave the example of how we learn math. Typically, we're taught theories, which are mainly concerned with exceptions to the rules, as the main course. That is teaching it backwards. *Frontwards* would be to teach how the data were collected and the theorem created; how it was discovered, developed, grew. And then, how to apply it. And then, and only then, the exceptions. *Then* the exceptions might make sense.

We are taught management theories the same way. Backwards: theories and exceptions. We never really learn where they came from, why, or how they work with real people.

Stories are *learning frontwards*, Box was saying. Think about it. You watch human behavior. How people act. What makes them tick, turn on, do their best. Then you create a management theory from that. Well then, if the stories, the real people stuff, is what made the theory, then when you want someone to really understand that theory, you ought to tell the real stories that it came from. Right?

Stories ... Folktales ... Parables ... that's how we used to learn. We forgot that when we got more sophisticated. We skipped right over the front part. The stories are the reality that makes the theories. They are what real people understand. It is the *frontwards* way to teach and to learn.

So that is why this book is real stories about real people. We hope they help you connect the theories to your real work.

INTRODUCTION BY
LEE CHEANEY

We begin learning things right after we're born. As infants, we're like learning sponges. We immediately begin to condense, to store, to compile, to collate, to merge data and information. We draw on our learning as necessary, and we use what's stored as the foundation to understand new and more complex ideas.

We move into structured learning environments called schools, and we are taught, in disciplined ways, the things that we trust are important to know—things like math, and language, and science, and philosophy, and religion, literature, and chemical formulas, and algebra, and weather, and custom, and tradition. There are people who, for their gentleness and love of children, are chosen to take on the responsibility of getting us ready for the adult world, and especially to help us understand about contribution and quality of life and how it is important that our short time in this world have meaning and purpose.

All of this is great. It is a magnificent scheme. It is survival of a species and a knowledge and a wisdom. But no one ever teaches us the raw dynamics of leading.

We watch and emulate our parents and teachers and idols. Many of us take the path of least resistance through college, through relationships, through jobs, and through life. Some of us are *Harvardized* or *Stanfordized* or *MBAed*. Then, we set ourselves loose in the workplace.

Suddenly, one day we find ourselves sitting at desks in offices and other people are looking to us for ideas and decisions and guidance. We feel like we know what we are doing. For the most part, we don't. *We don't even know that we don't know*. We often don't understand that we have a fear of leadership. We don't know how to lead. We are afraid to ask about it. We're supposed to already know. But from where is this knowledge supposed to come?

I talked recently to a "management team" of six people. We were having a very civil, working-breakfast in an expensive hotel. I took a risk and told "us" that we have an awesome responsibility. I tried to remind us that whether we like it or not, we have an effect on the way over 800 people feel when they wake up in the morning and when they go to bed at night. We, as leaders in the work place, influence the way husbands talk to wives, the way parents treat children, the way children feel about themselves and the way our kind decides to treat and talk and feel about each other. I told them, "That, my friends, is scary, and we need to take this seriously."

As I write, I realize that this book is a piece about life, and human interaction, and how we relate to each other, and how our responsibility and creativity are interwoven, and probably, how our effect on the people we are leading is beyond comprehension. The things we do and say at work are massively significant, even if we don't mean for them to be. My friend and co-author, Maury Cotter, spoke about the "domino effect," and how small things have large influence. We have to realize and accept the truth in that statement. That's responsible leading—not mindless reacting.

She said, "In school, we're taught to hang onto the rope and to make sure we keep our place in line." We are impressionable kids when we are taught or shown that important skill. People, mostly teachers, say these kinds of things to us, and we begin to absorb the concepts and ideas and thoughts they present. And then we make instant, tiny-kid decisions about how we are going to position ourselves in life—and in reality.

These are big ideas. These are important responsibilities. We can't take these ideas lightly. When I have the courage to stand up and say these things, I worry that people will see me as scheming, and think that I'm doing this for my own selfish purposes. I hope that I'm able to push those suspicions aside. That's the reason for this book. We've written simple stories to get your attention—to grab your thinking—to influence your behavior and your deciding.

Please read—and please contact us to tell us about your thoughts.

(Editor's Note: You can always reach Lee and Maury by writing to SPC Press, Inc.. Our address is on the copyright page.)

QUALITY—
THE KEY ELEMENTS

A great statistician named George Box once said, "You know, there are things like Mom and apple pie and the flag, and then there are things that people argue about. Well, Quality is like Mom and apple pie. It isn't something to argue about."

That pretty much sums up how we feel about what the world is calling Quality, or TQM, or TQL. Quality is not something to argue about. We don't have time for those arguments in our companies. Folks, *Quality is Market Survival*. Xerox is learning that. So is Ford and Harley Davidson and Campbell Soup and AT&T—and I could go on and on.

Quality is getting really close to the customers—all of them, and giving them what they really want—as close to when they really want it—as we can.

Quality is working together to really understand who the customers are *inside* our companies. Understanding who your customers are is easy. Look at what you are doing at any point in time. Who are you doing it for? Who touches that piece of work next—that document, that form, that letter, that phone message, that computer, that what-ever? That's your customer. You better be talking to that person—and often. You have to talk to your customers because Quality is what *they* want and need— not what *you* think they need—or what's convenient for you to deliver.

I said that Quality is working together. I mean *really* working together, not just working in the same building or in the same company, but in the true sense of working together in mature and spirited teams.

We Americans are an interesting lot. "I've always been a team player," we say. Malarkey! We think tossing a group of people into a room with a job to be done or a problem to be solved is a team. It's not. Teamwork takes time. Trust among members has to be built and safety has to be assured—and felt. A group of people cannot truly work effectively and efficiently if they do not trust each other. Teamwork maximizes participation, information and creativity. Teamwork is rich, rewarding and sat-isfying.

Quality is the integration of the fundamental building blocks of anything that happens. It is understanding that everything is a process—made up of tasks that can be con-tinuously studied and improved. It is seeing how pro-cesses are linked together to form systems and realizing that it is the system, or the process—not the people working in the system—that influences the characteristics of the product or the service.

It is the belief that people want to do a good job, and when they don't, it is likely that the system is getting in their way: perhaps the system is flawed or a process is inadequate. We don't make mistakes on purpose. We make mistakes in our worlds of work, generally, because of the system. We weren't trained properly or enough. The tools we have to use are slow or wrong. There are delays when systems require multiple approvals and signatures. But unfortunately, in most cases, when things go wrong, people are blamed and flawed systems go unchanged.

Quality is decision-making driven by data and fact, not by guesswork, intuition, opinion and emotion. It is understanding that our most important questions are simple ones like, "How do you know that?" "How are you going to find out?" and statements like, "Show me the data." Quality is an understanding and respect for the power of statistical thinking. Quality is, as Dr. Box has said, "taking statistics out of the classroom and into the boardroom where it belongs."

Sounds simple—and it is. But it takes time. It takes a shift in traditional business thought. It requires our companies to change. It requires education and training. It all takes time. It requires patient money. It requires persistence. It requires leadership and commitment and energy because it is not a "quick fix." It will not happen overnight.

THE STORIES

ONE . . .

Quality is a comprehensive approach to the organization and the design of work processes. It is a way to think about stuff. It's a way to treat each other. It's a way to constantly improve everything we lay our hands on.

ALMOND MUFFINS

This is a very small story about a big concept.

I was doing some work for the Federal Office of Personnel Management in Denver. I like to eat breakfast, so I told the waitress that I would like a ton of fresh fruit, a lot of coffee, and a bran muffin. "We're out of bran," she says, "but we have some almond muffins back there."

Almond muffins. I thought that sounded pretty interesting. My friend, Rob, thought almond muffins sounded interesting too, so we both ordered them.

In a few minutes, I got a big plate of fruit—all kinds—and both Rob and I got a bread plate with two warm brown muffins, sitting in that muffin paper just covered with slivered toasted almonds. We also got some nice little squares of butter wrapped in gold paper.

Soon, it was time for me to eat one of the muffins. I could tell Rob was getting ready for muffins too, because he had brushed all the slivered almonds off one of them and was removing the paper. "Great," says Rob. "Poppy seed." What? Poppy seed in my almond muffins? Sure enough, my almond muffin was a poppy seed muffin just wearing some almonds on top. I wasn't at all disappointed because I really like poppy seed anything. (It reminds me of my whole-earth college days of poppy seed stuff and brown rice and homemade yogurt and mung bean sprouts growing in a jar under the sink.)

I said this was a little story about a big concept. It is about variation. We all need to be careful to call things by the right name. And sometimes, we need to decide together what that name is.

If, in our workplaces, we use a bunch of different names for the same thing, it will throw the data out of whack. For instance, the person who makes muffins in that restaurant doesn't have any idea how many poppy seed muffins to make tomorrow—or any day for that matter. The muffin process is out of control. The customers aren't making decisions about poppy seeds; they are making decisions about almonds. The customers who order a muffin aren't going to get what they ordered. Biting into the muffin will be a surprise for most people. I suspect some will think that they got the wrong muffin. Others, perhaps those allergic to poppy seeds, will be really mad. Of course, if I order an almond muffin tomorrow, I will be just fine, because I really like poppy seeds. But being a customer these days is sometimes a real detective adventure.

The next day, in the same hotel, I asked what kind of

muffins they had "back there." "We have English muffins," she said. "Don't you have any bran muffins or something like that?" I asked. "Well," she pondered out loud, "I think there's a poppy seed one with some almonds on it."

Shucks, that adventure is over.

INVISIBLE STAR

Helen had worked at a golf club in Colorado Springs ever since it opened. She was a waitress—one of the best.

Helen knew about something that a lot of us don't. She knew about customers and how their needs have to be thought about and figured out. She taught me how to anticipate customers' needs, how to be quiet and polite and unobtrusive, how to handle children so the parents could enjoy their meals and their time in the club, and how to hold my temper when customers were unfair. She had to know those things because "tips" were important. The club only paid her minimum wage, and that isn't much when you have a 17-year-old daughter looking forward to the prom and college and life after that.

The people who owned the golf club wanted to be successful. Lots of money went into the landscaping and the furniture and the circular staircases that cascaded into banquet rooms, their floors covered with rich, burgundy carpeting. In all this luxury, the boss would chat with his buddies openly about Helen, and their other serving staff

—even while they were in the room—as if they were pets or maybe just furniture.

Late one night, after the customers were gone, while I (a busboy at the time) was pulling the dishes from the banquet room, Helen sat down at the piano to play a Chopin polonaise—because she knew I loved it. The boss heard the piano and came down the circular stairs. "Somebody must have been goofing off," he thought. There was work to be done. So Helen stopped the majestic music that was making my work more pleasant, and we pulled the rest of the dishes and the dirty linen.

The night had been good for the club. Customers had been happy. They had been lined up waiting for tables, and the boss and his buddies had congratulated each other on being successful. One of Helen's regular customers had given her a card with money in it, and a note that said, "You have always gone out of your way for us. If you ever leave this club, please be sure to tell us where you're working. We only come here because of you. Here's our phone number."

Helen tucked the card in her purse, thanked me for helping her, and left to go home. I would have liked for her to stay awhile and play more music, but she was tired and wanted to see if her daughter had had a good day.

When Helen finally quit for another job, I left too. I quit

the day I heard she was leaving. On Mother's Day that year, the big boss called my house and asked for help. The customers were in lines, and the serving staff wasn't very pleasant, and he was worried about the business.

FIVE STAR ASSOCIATE

Gayle works at a hotel in San Ramon, California. It was two days before Thanksgiving; she came to turn down the bed and lay wrapped chocolates on the pillow.

Gayle had a brass name badge that had five, bright stars on it. I asked about the badge.

"I'm a five star associate," she said, and she told me about the stars. She told me that you get a star if someone notices that you've done something special for them. Anyone can nominate you for a star—a hotel customer, or another associate, a peer, an internal customer. The stars become your proof of caring service, and you are proud to get them.

While Gayle talked and I listened, I thought it strange that the conversation seemed amazing.

Here was a customer of a splendid hotel—a hotel all dressed up for the holidays—being talked to by the person who came to turn down the bed, and she talked about management style and how it affected her and how she felt. She talked about her colleagues and how they all worked together and how they were excited. We talked about how she loved her job, and her friends, and the hotel. After a point she said, "I'm sorry. I have to go now. It has been nice talking to you."

I found one of the customer comment cards that are in most places these days. I filled it out. I took some time. I told the truth.

A week later, I got a letter from the manager of that hotel in San Ramon. I could tell it wasn't a form letter. The manager thanked me for taking the time to fill out the little yellow card. He told me how he appreciated all the associates that worked with him in that splendid hotel. He talked with pride about his team, and he gave me the 800 phone number to call direct to his office for reservation help if I wanted to stay with them again.

It was a nice, unusual experience. If ever I go to San Ramon again, I will stay there—even if it costs more.

PANTYHOSE—

RUNS IN THE CHARTS

I am buying a lot more pantyhose lately.

I have visions of corporate executives in board rooms patting themselves on the back while ogling over charts that point upward.

Maybe they're happy about the new ad campaign that shows how beautiful women wearing their pantyhose can work all day and dance all night.

Or maybe the executives are happy because the company started to use some new materials, and they think people like the new material even better and are buying more pantyhose.

But those aren't the reasons I am buying more pantyhose. I am buying more pantyhose because lately, I have been getting more runs in them.

As I write this, I am wearing a pair with a run that goes over my big toe, just about to peek out of where my shoe hides it. There is also a run going down my right leg, just to the edge of my skirt   When either one makes it into public view, I will buy a new pair of pantyhose.

This same brand rarely used to run. I haven't changed brands yet because I like the way they fit and because I know exactly which shelf in my regular store has them. They always have my size and my color and they have them at a good price. It is so convenient.

But I am tired of these runs. And it is getting expensive. Soon I will get up the initiative to find a new brand on a new shelf with a new sizing system and a new color range, and I will begin buying them instead. I will adapt.

I suspect that I am not the only one.

And then, all of a sudden, the corporate executives will watch the arrows on their charts take a dive, and they'll start guessing why.

I wish they would ask me, their customer, why I am buying more pantyhose now. I wish they wouldn't assume it's because I like their new ads or their new materials.

I wish they would make long-term decisions about some good materials that work. I would gladly pay more.

Short-term gains often result in long-term losses—especially when you aren't talking to your customers or when you aren't gathering the right data.

By the way—I am also buying more nail polish to put on my runs to slow the running process. I wonder how the corporate executives of the nail polish company are analyzing that data.

What would a product or service be like
. . . if it were perfect?

THE GUY IN THE BOX

IN THE LOBBY

I went to a big insurance company one day in downtown Milwaukee to give a speech to about a hundred of their managers. When I walked into their building, I found myself in a little city with all kinds of stuff going on at the same time.

There was a raised platform set up like a stage, and there were actors with loud resonant voices acting out a play. A few people were watching this—some sitting in chairs and some just standing around. There was a long table covered with big cream puffs being served to people by happy ladies with hair nets and white dresses. There was a round pool of water in the middle of this enormous lobby, and there were up-and-down escalators and elevator banks. There were lots of people walking and talking and looking pretty happy. It seemed festive.

There was also a guy sitting in a big box. I guess it was the customer or visitor information station. This guy in the box was not looking real festive. He looked frightened. Three people were trying to talk to him at the same time.

One fellow, a visitor, was "signing in" on a visitor register and asking the guy in the box a lot of questions. A woman, an employee in the building, was explaining that she had left her employee identification badge at home and needed a temporary one. She was reaching into the box rummaging around trying to get a badge as she talked. Another woman was just standing there looking mad at the guy in the box.

I walked up to the box and waited for my turn. While I waited, several others came to join me at the box. Eventually the guy in the box got to me. I signed the register and got a badge. I asked him to get in touch with Beth Grant. He asked, "Does she work in this building?" I said, "Yes." He said, "Do you have her number?" I said, "No, don't you?" He then pulled out a huge computer print-out, rummaged through it, and found Beth's number. He called to ask her to meet me and gave me instructions to take the escalator to the "bridge."

That little event is what Karl Albrecht calls a "moment of truth." Good or bad, valid or not, I got an impression about that company—right there in the lobby—through that process with the guy in the box.

Later that same day, I told the one hundred or so managers that some of them ought to just go down and watch the guy in the box. I told them that sitting in that box is an extremely difficult and important job. Whoever has that job has to deal, one-on-one, with hundreds of customers every day, and they should have every possible tool they need to help them with that critical function.

I wanted to tell those leaders in that corporate dining room up in the sky to put down their linen napkins and the forks with prime rib and go down and look around in their own lobby. I wanted to tell them to go find out what it's like to work in that big building.

Leaders need to know that stuff. They need to look, ask, and listen to their employees. They need to see their organizations through the eyes of their customers and the eyes of their workers. Because that is where the work is. And that is where the organization works . . . or doesn't.

Image is perception.
You manage perception by managing moments of
truth. It's a process.

Two . . .

OWNING THE FIX

I was a rookie analyst in 1974. Right out of college, a "trainee." My job was to fix problems in workflow, manual systems, procedures, forms, etc.. Someone would identify a problem and send me in to fix it.

Usually the identifier of the problem was someone from outside of the "problem work" area. This meant that the people in the problem work area were labeled as less than adequate. Into this situation I was sent—a rookie analyst, who knew nothing about their programs, to "fix it."

They saw me coming—a 24 year-old, 5'2", blonde "girl." They were veterans of their programs. They developed them from infancy. Dedicated years of service—doing the best job they knew how. The value of their lives wrapped around their profession and the work they were doing— the work that was now publicly identified as a "problem."

The measure of my success would be to identify the causes of the problem and fix them—fast—and move on to the next problem somewhere else.

The measure of success of the people with the problem was to either prove there was no problem—or—to prove it was unfixable.

Our goals were at odds from the beginning. Someone was going to win and someone was going to lose.

Then I was assigned a project to look at the problem of numerous errors in a payroll system. I decided to look for a way to make this situation win-win.

This story has characters. Sharon was the head of the agency's payroll unit. She was a large, high-strung, aggressive woman, late 50's, with a booming voice. She was absolutely dedicated to getting checks out on time and accurately. Her integrity and self-esteem depended on it.

Carla was in her mid-30's, moderately aggressive, persistent, and also dedicated to doing a good job. All the payroll data from the field offices went to Carla's unit, which processed it, and sent it all to Sharon's unit.

There were always discrepancies between the two units. And whenever there was a discrepancy, everyone had to stop and figure out which was right—and which was wrong—and they had to do it fast, or the checks would be late. You knew it was the Wednesday before payday when you heard Sharon in the halls tracking down errors on foot. And things were always lost between the two units. Each accusing the other of having it and each keeping logs on what they received from whom when and what they sent when to whom—or whatever.

Jane, another rookie analyst, was assigned to work with me. Our assignment: to fix it. We began with interviews—loud, accusing, mad, not a lot of facts or data. Their goal: to prove the other unit was at fault.

Then we decided to try out a new way of doing our job. These two women knew their work. They really knew the system. We could have spent days and weeks gathering and documenting, and we would never have learned what they already knew about the process.

So we decided to use their knowledge and their energy and channel it into fixing the problem. We reserved a conference room for two mornings. We put in a coffee pot, rolls, a flip chart, and markers. We began with a warm-up game to help loosen the tension. Then we talked about how they knew the process and the work better than we could ever hope to. And that we wanted to guide them in fixing their own problem.

We started by flowcharting the existing system, step-by-step, forms being completed, sent, filed, copied, added to, sent back, received, stamped, logged, etc.. We were beginning to identify some areas of duplication. It seemed that it would be easy to then identify which unit should do that step, eliminate that step in the other unit, and start to solve the problem. Things were looking very promising. We had hit on a new way to do our jobs: to involve the workers in improving their own jobs.

Then something happened. One of them said something offensive, and the other responded in true form and they were off and yelling at each other. Jane and I tried to intervene with some order, but couldn't be heard over the roar. We sat back and looked at each other—Naive Rookies. Now what should we do?

We just listened for awhile. Then we started to hear something else happen. It was hard to hear at first, but it seemed like some order was coming out of the hurricane of emotions. We asked some leading questions, wrote down and drew what they were saying, and listened.

Yes, there was duplication. Lots of duplication. Indeed, it was all duplication. Carla's unit duplicated Sharon's unit. Everything Carla's unit did was done again in Sharon's unit. There was no reason for Carla's unit. That was the conclusion that Sharon *and Carla* reached. We asked lots of testing questions, drew pictures and flow charts, played devil's advocate; and it seemed the idea was sound.

The four of us then went to my boss and tested it on him. He listened, also tested it, and was also convinced.

So we wrote it up in a report. The report was from the four of us. Both Carla and Sharon signed it. They both came to the meetings with management to explain and "sell" the recommendation. It was accepted. They both worked hard to implement it effectively. Carla's job was eliminated. She had rights to other jobs in the agency, and moved on to grow in her new job.

The new system worked better and faster than the old system and freed up thousands of hours of time. Two positions were able to be cut through attrition, ultimately benefitting the taxpayer, without anyone losing their job.

They understood it. They owned it. They made it happen. We *all* won.

CROSSING LINES
AND PARADIGMS

A problem: "It takes too long to evaluate transcripts and calculate the grade point average (GPA) for students applying to graduate school."

"Why is that a problem?"

"Because we can't offer a student admission until we have the cumulative GPA."

"Why is that a problem?"

"Other universities do it faster and can offer students admission sooner."

"Why is that a problem?"

"We are not getting our best shot at attracting top students. They're going to the schools they hear from earlier, not waiting to hear from us."

"What is the current system?"

"When a student applies to graduate school, the university requires a copy of transcripts from all colleges previously attended."

"Why is that a problem?"

"It takes too long to get them all in."

"Why?"

"Different schools get them in at different times, and the cumulative GPA can't be calculated until they are all in."

"Why do we require all those transcripts?"

"Because the university departments want them."

"Are you sure?"

"We surveyed the departments and they said, 'We want them *all* and we want them *fast*'—just as we expected."

But a month later, someone asked again: "Why do they want all those transcripts?"

So we asked, "Why do you want them?" And the departments said, "Well, the fellowship programs want all the transcripts."

"Fellowships, why do you want them?"

"We don't," they said. "We thought Graduate Admissions required them. Quit sending us all that stuff."

We are changing the system so the GPA calculation is based on transcripts from the last two years of undergraduate school.

Fewer transcripts mean fewer pieces of mail to wait for, fewer pieces to process, fewer pieces to look up and match, and fewer pieces to calculate.

People in this process didn't know what others in the process did or needed. People were thinking about the work they did as being in containers drawn by the organization chart. People didn't communicate across the process.

We stepped out of the containers, crossed the organizational lines, and took a look at the whole process.

Then we stepped out of a bigger container. We asked other schools how they processed transcripts and found one that broke a paradigm about having to calculate the GPA's for all applicants. We found that we could have the departments screen applicants and tell us which ones needed to have GPA's calculated, cutting the number to process at least in half.

It used to take an average of 26 days for the graduate school to complete their part of the process. With the improvements, it appears that the time will be cut to about three days.

It's good to find the customers in every process
and talk to them.

COACHING SOCCER

Ian used to be a professional soccer player. When he made a play and it worked, his coach said, "Good job." Sometimes he made the same play and it didn't work and then his coach would say, "Don't do that. You aren't trying hard enough." Ian was frustrated and confused.

Then he went to college and majored in statistics. He learned about variation. He learned how to use statistics to degrees of complexity that lose most of us. He can tell you how to experiment and calculate and project so that you can build a mold "wrong," so that when the hot stuff gets poured in and changes the shape of the mold, the resulting shape will be right—perfectly right.

He earned his Ph.D. in statistics at the University of Wisconsin. As he was learning these methods, he recognized another application: soccer.

Ian took this knowledge and helped coach two high school soccer teams. He began by asking, "What is our measure of success?" Simple. Winning the most games. Then he said, "How do we win the most games?" You get the most goals and you lose the fewest. "How do we get goals?" "How do we lose goals?" The kids listed the ways. They identified penalty kicks as one of the most significant ways they could make goals. So they concentrated on how to improve their chance of scoring with penalty kicks.

They needed to identify the best penalty kicker. The coach didn't just pick the person who made the great goal last week, because he understood variation. They designed and conducted a controlled experiment to identify the best kicker. The resulting player surprised the coach and the players. The player even surprised himself. (But he did have the biggest feet.) He proved to be the best kicker over time as they kept ongoing data.

They also constructed an experiment to see where it was most effective to aim crossing kicks. The kids thought it would be right to the middle of the goal. Through the process of the experiment, they learned that a greater percentage of goals are made when you kick it to the opposite corner of the goal. The data spoke clearly and the kids understood.

They learned that one good kick, or one bad kick, didn't mean anything. In the presence of variation, you need to collect and interpret data in a meaningful way to understand and make sound decisions. Ian and his team now understood what he and his coach hadn't years ago.

One of his teams, a girl's team, was having trouble with "heading" the ball. Ian kept them practicing, but the more they practiced the worse they got. He was about to give up. He was beginning to think that maybe they weren't trying hard.

Then one day before practice, one of the girls asked him if they were going to practice heading. He said, "Yes." And she said, "Okay," ran over to her bag, took something out, and swallowed it. Ian asked her what she just took. She said, "Aspirin." She knew her head was going to hurt. At first, he laughed. Then he decided it wasn't funny. They *were* trying. They were trying very hard.

He went home and diagrammed the process of heading. He broke it down to six process steps: anticipate, run, jump, bend at the waist, snap, head the ball. Then he designed a drill for each step. He learned that the girls were struggling with the snap step. They were just crashing into the ball with their body force. No wonder it hurt! The drill he designed was done while sitting, so only the snapping motion could be used and thereby, strengthened.

Three weeks later, another coach remarked to him on how good his team was at heading.

The two teams Ian coached outdid their historic records that year. One went to regional competition and the other went to the state finals.

One of the teams was an underdog among the eight state finalists. For the first two games, the score was 0-0 in the regulation time. They won both games by penalty shoot-outs. Five minutes before the end of the championship game, their opponents made the only goal of the game, yet Ian's team still won the "Team of the Week" award in Wisconsin.

I had heard about Ian's success with soccer teams. And I was giving a talk on teamwork that week. So I asked him to my house to hear about teamwork. But he told me about process, variation, and data.

I learned from Ian the power of the integration of the principles of teamwork and scientific method. One supports the other. Together they produce results.

TAKE OFF YOUR COAT

AND HAVE A SEAT

Passengers grew anxious while their plane was sitting on the run-way, waiting for a place to park. The flight was already late when it arrived because it was late leaving. Now it would be difficult at best for some of the passengers to make important connections to their final destinations. Passengers vented their anger at the attendants. Flight attendants apologized but could do nothing.

This was a common occurrence for this major airline. For years, top management had wrestled with the problem. Flights were generally on schedule and passengers were happy during the spring, summer and fall months. But during the winter, delays were common. The delays caused numerous problems. Customers had to have new tickets issued, often on other airlines, because of missed connections. Baggage was misrouted. There were scenes in airports between angry, frustrated customers and hassled ticket agents.

Management tried to solve the problem. They believed it was the weather that extended the ground time for the planes. But it wasn't the in-flight time that was causing the delays; it was the time the planes were spending on the ground. Ground time was unpredictable.

So, management of the airline worked with management of the airport to share the expense of new snow removal and plane de-icing equipment. There was no change. The delays continued. An expensive solution had no effect.

Was it lighting problems? New ground lights were installed. Was it ground crew problems? Ground crews were evaluated and timed on their activities, which of course, angered the ground crews. These were more, costly attempts at solving the problem, but there were still delays.

The flight attendants knew the answer to the problem. But no one asked them for their ideas. When they attempted to give their opinion, top management never heard them.

The problem was coats. All the passengers wear coats on winter flights, especially those flights to or from snowy cities. When all the passengers wear coats, it takes longer for them to board the plane as well as get off. Passengers would stand in the aisle removing coats, folding them, and placing them in overhead compartments. The aisles would get clogged. Bottlenecks would occur. The plane couldn't back out of its berth on time and the next plane couldn't come in. Over the course of each wintry day, the effect of the delays multiplied, resulting in numerous late planes, missed schedules, misrouted bags, and angry customers.

The flight attendants had observed this at the start and end of each flight. They had ideas and information. They tried to pass them on. But management wasn't listening.

INVOLVE ME,
I'LL UNDERSTAND

If *you tell me, you won't convince me. If you show me, you may convince me. If you involve me, I'll understand.*

The legislature approved a new program with four positions to begin an effort to locate and upgrade underground petroleum storage tanks in the state. Most of the existing tanks were installed in the 1950's and were now rusted through and leaking, posing a threat to the groundwater supply. The new program was to be located in the division of Safety and Buildings where I worked as an analyst. It was not yet decided in which bureau it would be located.

The issue of *which* bureau was not as clear as you might expect. There were three bureaus whose missions overlapped with the mission of the new program: Plumbing, Technical Services, and Petroleum Inspection. So where should this new program and positions be located?

The division administrator asked a young, smart man in

the Plumbing Bureau to write a report and make a recommendation. He did. As soon as it hit the copy machine, smoke and rumors flew everywhere. "What does he know about our program? Why should he make the recommendation? He didn't even talk to me." Every possible error he made was pointed out and magnified.

I asked the division administrator if we could pull together a team to evaluate the options and make a recommendation. He agreed.

We set up two consecutive mornings and a conference room. We invited each bureau director, the man who wrote the report, and a couple of other involved people.

We began by defining and outlining the new program. What was it? What was the mission? What were all the tasks and functions? What portion of the four positions would be doing each task and function? Who would the customers be? Who would be monitoring and interfacing with the program externally and internally?

Then we looked at each of the three existing bureaus in much the same way.

We wrote it all down on flip charts with diagrams and lists. We taped it all over the walls of the room, so we could all see it at the same time. That's about as far as we got the first morning. It was good to step away at that point and digest the material overnight.

The next morning, we resumed. We listed organization alternatives. Then we took the list of new program functions, one by one, and talked about where they best fit. By lunch time, we had reached a consensus about where the program and positions best fit, complete with supporting rationale.

That afternoon, we wrote the new report. The "by-line" was everyone in that room. They all signed the report. It was delivered to the division administrator. He approved it. It was implemented with support, instead of noise and dissent.

And now the rest of the story. . .

That final report was nearly identical to the one the young, smart man from the Plumbing Bureau did in the first place.

Some people reading this will say, "Well, then, you wasted two days."

The rest of you will get it.

THREE . . .

SARA—

DOING THE WRONG STUFF RIGHT

At one time, I believe I had one of the best people working for me that a boss could hope to have. Sara had been with the organization for many years. Nearly everyone knew her and knew of her loyalty and dedication. She was tireless. She never used the sick leave that she earned. We almost had to force her to take the vacation time she had coming at the end of each calendar year.

One day, I noticed that Sara was really grinding away at putting numbers on spreadsheet paper in a black three-ring binder. Sara was a hard worker. She prided herself in her excellent productivity and her impeccable accuracy. All that day she worked on that binder. She worked from large piles of computer printouts that were stacked around her. Her fingers were a blur as they flew over her adding machine.

I didn't get a chance to chat with Sara the first day I noticed her working on the binder. I only noticed because it wasn't a task I had seen her perform before. On the second day she was still busy, head bent over the black binder. I went over to her area. "Hi, Sara," I said. "What are you working on?"

"These are my stats," said Sara, and that started one of the most interesting conversations I had ever had with her. I asked if she pulled this data together for the monthly production schedules that ultimately came to me.

"No, these numbers don't go in those schedules," she replied.

"Oh," said I, "you must be pulling these numbers together to serve as a quick reference in answering the dozens of telephone calls you get each day."

"No," Sara explained, "I don't need the binder for them."

"Oh, you must run these tabulations for Roy, and then he uses them in his unit."

"No, these aren't used over there."

"Sara, who uses this binder?"

"I don't know."

"Do you keep this binder here in your area?"

"Yes."

"Does any one ever come here and look in this binder?"

"No."

"Sara, do you ever use the information in this binder?"

"Nope," said Sara.

In the next few moments, I learned about a complexity existing in one of the systems within my jurisdiction. Complexity is work or tasks that people do which do not add any value to the product or service the organization provides. *Complexity is not real work.* Sara told me proudly that she had gotten the length of time necessary to do these monthly tabulations down to two days. She told me she had been doing these tabulations and recording the results in the black binder for almost ten years. That's two days a month, twelve months a year for almost ten years.

When I asked her why she did this, she told me about a dead guy—a guy I had never met, but had heard of. Well, the guy had asked Sara, back when she worked for him, to pull together a certain kind of data in a black binder because he had a hunch that another party might call and ask for the numbers and he wanted to be prepared—just in case. Then he died. He never told her to stop. Neither did anyone else. Sara would have trained her replacement to do this task, and the organization would never have been able to find out why it was being done. That's complexity; that's not real work.

At one time, Sara knew who her customer was. Her customer was that manager who had given her the original assignment. But Sara hadn't been taught the importance of staying close to her customers. Her original customer was gone. She hadn't been instructed to continually talk with her customers about her work activities—if she had, she would have stopped working on the numbers in the black binder years before our conversation.

Sara was doing things right. She was accomplishing the task perfectly. There was never a doubt about Sara's accuracy, speed, and dependability. But she wasn't doing the right work.

It wasn't Sara's fault. She hadn't been told to continually question whether the things she did were the right things to do for her customers.

DEAR BOSS

I told you I would tell you things that I believe you need to know—even if I suspect you might not like hearing what I have to say.

There is a great deal of tension in the company, and it isn't what I would call healthy tension. It is a tension building from a foundation of fear. I don't believe the fear is that the company is not going to "make it." The problem is that people in the company do not have enough trust to talk openly and honestly.

I realized earlier today that I was feeling funny—uncomfortable. I was busy on a variety of things, but the discomfort kept returning and it was troubling. I finally stopped and did an internal check. Was I starting to feel ill? Was something bothering me that hadn't yet emerged from my subconscious? Then I knew what it was. I was feeling a little afraid. I haven't felt that way in the world of work for years, and my tolerance for that feeling is extremely low.

The next step was to look for root causes. That was easy

because I have been spending the last couple of days collecting data. So I cancelled my trip to Washington because I felt doing this was much more important.

Here's the data.

I learned that an employee was "castrated"—as someone called it—because of a question he asked at one of the "all employee meetings." Did you know that? The reason for the "slap" was that the question was "stupid." When something like that happens, it has a multiplier effect. Not only will that employee be afraid to ever open his mouth again (provided he stays with the company), but everyone who hears the story will think twice before asking questions or making comments.

Is there such a thing as a "stupid" question? We've got to want to stop things like that from happening, and if they do happen, we need to attend to the people they happen to and then make sure they don't happen again.

I believe that people are afraid of management.

More data:

"...are you kidding—be accused of not being a team player, and get my head handed to me on a plate?" said one. What this means is that the employees don't have a clear understanding of what's being agreed to—or whether there is consensus. They aren't willing to take the risk of disagreeing. Some are, to some extent, but not all of them. If that potential problem, the "kill the messenger" syndrome, is a reality, we cannot achieve a Quality-driven environment. It can't happen in a culture which has that level of fear.

I worked for a guy a couple of years ago who took delight in scaring people. He was thrust upon me by a new governor. He put my Quality Improvement implementation efforts back six months. I am not suggesting that you want people to be afraid. On the contrary, I believe that you just didn't realize that our people might not be as trusting as they pretend.

There are other stories. Reports of people expressing honest opinions and as a result, falling from their boss's favor or suffering retribution. It is an element of our culture that is toxic—it is a "complexity" in our system of communication, innovation, and creativity. It hampers collaboration and cooperation.

The only person who can start to do anything about this is you, Boss. Want some help?

This issue has to be put on the table in a big way. This is important, and I am deadly serious. If this company is to pull together and tap its most valuable resource—its *people*—we've got to say loud and clear, "It is time to take a good look at the way we treat each other around here."

We have to learn to tolerate honest mistakes. But we also have to watch for and be intolerant of incompetence

The philosophy at a corporation I know of in Milwaukee is that people don't know when they are incompetent. That's called *unconscious incompetence*. Every leader in this company has to understand that it is a big part of their job to move their direct reports up the ladder, from unconscious incompetence to *unconscious competence*. That's where people operate perfectly—without even thinking about it. That's also called mastery. When we see our people operating at a level of unconscious competence, it's time to give them something new to do and start them up a new ladder. That's growing people—developing our resources. We have to believe it and do it.

Perception is reality . . .
            to the one who perceives it.

ONE WEEK OF RESPECT

My brother recently resigned to take a new job. He gave two weeks notice. After one week, management told him not to come back for his last week.

My brother had been a landscape architect for this major engineering firm for ten years. He worked long hours, traveled over 40,000 miles a year, and committed himself to doing a good job. He designed and helped land important contracts for the firm, including major marina developments and several projects in other states. He managed projects representing over $100,000 in professional fees at a time. In his ten years at the company, his salary increased by over 400%.

Lately, he was not so happy at work. It seemed like the guys at the top were out for themselves with no regard for him and his peers. It seemed he and his peers were expected to do all the work with no recognition or compensation. Heavy rumors about shake-ups kept everyone looking over their shoulders.

He was offered a new job with a small, innovative company. It was a bit of a risk, but offered excitement and challenge. The owners, smart creative people, valued him and went out of their way to get him. They offered him a job. He took it.

He announced his resignation on Monday and gave two weeks notice. On Friday afternoon, when most people had gone for the day, a new manager, green behind the ears, stopped by and told my brother it was best that he not come back to work anymore. He should take his personal belongings and not return on Monday for his last week.

Why do you think the manager would do this?

❋ *Maybe he thought my brother would spend this last week talking about his new job and making everyone else feel the grass was greener elsewhere and then they would all leave.*

Perhaps. But consider: If he talks about his new job, then everyone will realize that the work they are doing for this company is obviously valued by others on the outside. If people feel their work is important, they might even stay and do it longer.

❋ *He would spend the week gathering copies of everything he worked on to take with him.*

Well, maybe. But, if he were going to do that, he would have already gathered whatever he wanted to take.

*   *During the last week he might use his old contacts to bring them to his new business.*

If he were going to do this, he would do it anyway. If he is insulted by the company, he is, in fact, more likely to do it.

*   *He probably wouldn't be very productive anyway—that last week.*

So what. After ten years, what's one half-productive week?

Maybe I missed some big point to the value of getting him out of there one week early. I asked if they suspected him of anything unethical. He said he knew of nothing like that.

It seems there is an ego to many organizations; a mentality that expects you to give all of yourself. And if you leave, you have abandoned ship, and become an outcast. It's their ball and their rules.

Then the left cheek got hit. One week after he was sent home, he received a certified letter. It announced that his health insurance was already cancelled, as of the previous week. He had been left without insurance for two days—without any notification.

What did all this say to my brother? He worked for ten years—ten years—most of his waking hours. Major commitments—long days and nights—hard trips—designing and redesigning. His job was a major part of his life. He was proud of his work; it made him feel good about himself.

Then he is told to pack up right away, and that his insurance is cancelled. No one says, "Nice job designing the marina that was featured in a national magazine" or "Thanks for going to St. Paul every other week for two years to develop and manage two major projects there."

He does not feel valued. He feels no commitment to the place. When people ask him about his old job, they won't hear about a strong company that did great work.

How do his co-workers feel? They are still there, working for this engineering company. Long hours. Hard trips. Designing and redesigning under the direction of the big guys. Expected to be committed to their jobs. To the company. Expected to give their best time, most of their waking hours, their creativity to the job they are doing. Jobs that won't have their names on them.

And now they know that if they do this for ten years, it won't even amount to one week of respect!

Consider the value of all the knowledge in that company. Then try to figure out the cost of telling that one person to get out one week early.

When engineers, accountants, and other specialists, suddenly become managers of people, they should learn the art of working with people, just as they have learned the science of their profession. Because they now have a new job, a new field: *people*.

Leading people is different than designing a building or managing a complex account. It is a science and an art.

And it is knowing that a person deserves at least one week of respect.

UNCHAINED MELANY

John became a manager two years ago when he was 32. He was hired as the executive director of a small non-profit organization. The agency is in charge of monitoring and providing services to non-profit nursing homes around the state. He inherited three staff members.

In his first week on the job, he told each of his staff that he wanted to meet with them individually. He wanted to talk to them about what they do and what they wanted to do for the organization.

He expected simple encounters with history and facts. And that's what he got from two of the staff. The third person, Melany, knocked his socks off!

She came into the room for their meeting with stacks of papers in her arms and brimming with enthusiasm. She showed him ideas for conferences she wanted to organize, materials she wanted to develop, methods for making their publications look professional, and information they could capture and organize that would be useful to their

membership. She told him what she felt their membership was looking for and how, by providing those things,
she felt they could increase the size of their membership
significantly. She went on and on with her ideas—and
documents to illustrate them.

John was overwhelmed and apprehensive. Who was this
woman? Melany was the director of member services.
But her duties were almost 50% clerical functions. For 10
years she had been there—doing those things. Why
would she suddenly have all these ideas? He addressed
her ideas cautiously; not to commit to, or encourage over-
zealousness. He needed to check this out.

He proceeded with caution. He talked with a few folks
who had worked with her for years. He stepped through
some of her ideas with her, point by point, one by one, trying them out. He was convinced of the validity of some
of her ideas. He went to the Board and asked for money to
buy a computer and the software she needed. They
approved it so fast it shocked him.

Melany went to work on the computer. She began producing beautiful, professional flyers and reports. He gave
her more room and authority. She planned the best conference they had ever had. He gave her more room. She
took the notes from a strategic planning session and created a draft five-year plan for the agency. This time he
hired someone to type and answer the phone to give her

more room. She created the best year-end report the members had ever seen. They said, "If this is the kind of materials you provide, we will remain members forever." They told other agencies. Other agencies joined. Membership increased beyond any level in their history.

They are now collecting enough new money, through their increased memberships, to cover the cost of the computer they bought, the cost of the person who does Melany's phone answering and typing, and a deserved raise for Melany—with money to spare.

She has since gone on to address her vision of improving the image of long-term care. She raised money and developed public service announcements and promotions. They have received such positive response that eight other states are now using the ads.

Remember, Melany had been there for 10 years. She didn't suddenly just come up with these ideas. She'd had them all along. And she had tried to convince previous directors. But they told her there was already too much work to be done and the phone was ringing.

John gave her space, permission, tools, and encouragement.

The biggest risk might be not to take a risk!

ASK A KID

One evening, I was preparing to give a talk to an insurance company on teamwork. I stopped to talk with Adam, my nine-year-old son, and to tuck him into bed. Adam thought it was cool that I was going to give this talk the next day and wanted to know what I was going to talk about. I told him I was going to talk about working together in teams. I decided to ask him for some ideas. I asked if he could think of things I could tell them about why it was a good idea to work together in teams.

He pondered briefly, lying on his water bed, snuggling his old grey bear. Then he said, "Well, you can get done faster, because you are all working together."

"That's right, Adam," I said. "Can you think of any other reasons?"

He thought again, and said, "You can do better, because if you're all working together, you should agree on what you're working on."

I asked, "Why is that good if you all agree?"

He said, "Because, if you all agree, there is a better chance that you are right." BINGO!!

I grabbed a small piece of scrap paper and wrote it down. I told him that he had just said about all there was to say about teamwork, in a couple of powerfully simple sentences. He asked me how long I had to talk and I told him two hours. He got a painful, apprehensive look on his face and told me to talk real slow and pause a lot.

I opened and closed my talk the next day with Adam's quote, and I have been using it ever since. Adam gets royalties on his quote now. He wrote it out in his own handwriting for me. I reprinted it and made overhead foils. I use it to cover training packets on teamwork.

A management theorist developed the following points:

*   *Do the job right.*

*   *Do the right job.*

Not far from Adam's:

*   *You will get done faster, because you are all working together.*

*   *You will do better, because if you all agree, there's a better chance that you are right.*

Sometimes the most powerful ideas are the simplest.

Ask a kid.

> If you work in teams, you can:
>
> Get done faster-
> because you are all
> working together
>
> Do better-
> because if you all
> agree, there is a
> better chance that
> you are right.
>
> by Adam cotter
>   9 years old

FOUR . . .

RISKY DATA

Good data is at the heart of good management. But sometimes you need to examine the culture in order to accurately read the data.

We were doing a study on safety in our department. Workers' compensation records gave us data on reported injuries over the last three years. We broke down the data by division and type of injury. Then we stopped to analyze what we saw.

One division showed many more injuries than any other. And one division showed no injuries in the three-year period. We decided we had probably found a division where we should concentrate improvement efforts. And one where we could study and learn what methods had been employed to be successful at avoiding injuries.

In the division with the most injuries, we found significant risks and back strain involved with their job of inspecting grain in enormous grain elevators on the waterfront of Lake Superior. We also found a well-developed safety program. They had a safety officer and a safety manual. They had studied their injuries over the last few years and had provided safety equipment and training, and documented improvements. Employees were made aware of safety practices and encouraged to report injuries. And they did report them.

In the division with no injuries, there were also jobs with significant bodily risks. These people inspected farm animals for disease. We found they were often injured when handling healthy and sick animals. They were kicked, stepped on, bit, chased, and exposed to disease and medication.

A note on one survey form said, "When I first started this job, I got smashed between two cows, kicked in the *you-know-what*, fell on the ice, hurt my back wrestling a pig, and stuck with a needle full of animal antibiotics." And then the telling line: "I guess I finally got smart."

The division had no safety awareness or training program. And the culture that existed said, "You're a klutz if you get injured. And a wimp if you report it."

In this case, the report data alone would have led us down the wrong path in assessing and improving our safety program. We had to become familiar with the culture to learn the real facts.

A HARD STORY TO HEAR

I recently spent one day with a meat inspector. He works for the state and his job is to inspect and regulate meat plants for compliance with state and federal regulations in their processing of meat. I asked to see a "good" plant, a "bad" plant, and a "downer" plant.

A downer plant is one where cows who can no longer walk are sent. A more in-depth inspection of these animals is done to determine why they can't walk, which in turn, determines whether or not they will enter the human food chain. It is this visit that I will tell you about.

The plant was a small, plain building. We walked through a narrow office area with an old desk littered with papers, ragged posters on the wall, and blood stained white coats hanging on a rack. From there, we entered a room. It was cold and damp. Three men were there, talking and laughing. All wore bloody, white coats and hard hats. The room was square—about 20 by 20 feet. In the corner hung a cow, upside-down. Two of the men were slashing a cut from end to end, from which warm blood gushed and the internal organs fell into a wheelbarrow.

The third man, the inspector, examined the internal organs with his plastic-gloved hands, looking for signs of infection, cancer, or other reasons why the cow could not walk.

That first cow showed no signs of problems internally. She did have bruised muscles in one of her hind legs. It was apparent that the reason she could not walk was due to a leg injury. They indicated that this is the most common cause for downer animals, which proved true in the time I was there. The inspector passed the cow for entry into the food chain.

Meanwhile, the two men continued their process, skinning and beheading. They were crude fellows, wielding sharp butcher tools with flare, making the kind of jokes that were probably necessary to remain sane in such a job.

Once a cow was "finished," a man went into a connected room and I followed. It was a much larger area, with overhead doors to the outside. It was full of cows, all lying down. He attached a chain to one of the cow's hind legs and pressed a pipe-like instrument to her head. I heard a muffled sound and the dead cow went up in the air, upside-down, and the process began again.

Let's talk about the job of this inspector for a minute. He

has a Ph.D. in veterinary medicine. His job is to inspect these animals to ensure they are safe for human consumption. He stands in that cold room all day, rummaging through warm guts—to do that job. And what happens if he finds a problem that condemns that animal for human consumption? He tells the other two guys in the room that they can't sell that animal. Those two guys lose money for each animal they can't sell.

Who is the customer of the inspector? Who does he serve? Answer: *you and me*—the consumers. We will eat whatever he passes.

But the answer doesn't stop there. The plant owners and operators are also his customers. Through his guidance they meet regulations, stay in business, and provide safe food for us, the consumers.

Who does this inspector work with, day in and day out? The owners and operators. He does not work with his ultimate customer, the consumer. He does not work with peers. He sometimes sees his supervisor.

So now, the next cow is processed. The inspector finds an infection. He tells the others that this animal cannot be sold.

Most plant owners are not happy with this news. They lose money. Sometimes they think the decision is border line; excessive. They sometimes try to influence the decision. Most meat plant owners and operators realize food safety is important to their business, and they willingly and respectfully comply. Our department records indicate, however, that this is not always the case. Inspectors are sometimes intimidated, harassed, threatened, or assaulted if they say an animal cannot be sold.

If the inspector has a problem, he should report it to the department, which will commence with administrative and/or legal action. The department has indicated its commitment to backing inspectors in these cases. The process is slow.

Sometimes the inspector does not report such incidents. Or he is unsure of the department's backing or worried that reporting the incident will only make things worse.

Sometimes the inspectors are embarrassed; they feel they somehow should have been able to avoid the incident.

Some inspectors are not completely innocent; they abuse their power, overzealous in their mission.

Imagine for a moment that you are an inspector. You identify a cow that has an infection and should not be entered into the human food chain. The owner objects. He calls you names and points his knife at you in a threatening way. He "accidentally" spills a pail of blood on your shoes and pants. These actions are not ones that would make much of a case for legal action.

Your job is to be there all day, tomorrow, and to continue to be there two days every week. Your peers are in other plants. Your supervisor is in the office. You are alone.

Your job is to ensure safe food to the consumers. The consumers are happy at home eating hamburgers. They don't know you, or even about you.

Most inspectors learn to handle these situations. They learn to deal with the people and the problems. They believe in their mission and they do the best job they know how. The best job involves quality inspection with interaction and guidance to the plant, and firm regulation. When they do their best work, the consumer wins, the plant wins, the taxpayer wins, and the inspector wins.

As consumers, we need to appreciate the jobs people like meat inspectors, police officers, building inspectors, and others do for us everyday. We need to encourage and recognize the value and importance of quality in government services.

Leaders in these areas have a big job. Quality leadership principles are tested to the maximum in these jobs. At the same time, the principles are needed here more than ever.

These meat inspectors need to feel part of a team. They need to know they are not alone.

They need to feel safe and trusted by their supervisor, so that they can go to them when they have a problem.

They need to be involved in program and policy decisions because only they know what is really going on in the program.

They need to understand *exactly who their customers are* to understand the complexities and priorities of their jobs.

They need resources, tools, and training to do their jobs.

They need to know strategies for working with people in this complex environment, as well as the technical skills of the job.

They need to feel recognized and appreciated. They need to know that someone knows and cares that they stick their necks out to protect the safety of people they don't know.

As consumers, we have a responsibility to be aware.

As leaders, we have a responsibility to build quality principles into these, and all jobs.

It's better to have BIG BROTHER
standing next to my shoulder
than to be looking over it.

Working Hard

and

Falling Behind

We had a program in our department that was 32 weeks behind in processing. People who installed alternative energy systems in their homes could apply for a refund from our agency. We reviewed, and then approved or denied each application. If approved, they got a refund.

A team was formed to try to get the program caught up. The team consisted primarily of the workers in the unit.

They made process improvements, and they were working hard to catch up, but it wasn't enough. They were actually getting further behind as time went on.

They examined the current process and collected data. How were they processing the applications? What did they spend their time doing?

They found that a lot of time was spent on two activities:

*   Generating letters to applicants to say their applications would be processed in about 30 weeks.

*   Answering phone calls from angry applicants who had been waiting up to 30 weeks.

Both of these activities were completely unnecessary. It was like all the time airlines spend finding and returning lost luggage—unnecessary work—if they didn't lose the luggage in the first place. . . .

Work that adds no value. Complexity.

They hired engineering students for six weeks and taught them how to process the routine applications. The experienced staff then concentrated on the more difficult applications. Six weeks later, the program was caught up so they were processing applications received that week.

They were able to stop generating the letters to applicants telling them how long they would have to wait.

And with fewer angry applicants, the phone rang a lot less often.

Instead of coping with angry clients, the staff was free to do real work.

ANNE SHIRE GOT FIRED

Anne got fired yesterday. I know there are always two sides to every story. I only know one in this case—Anne's. I would like to know the other side, but I'm hesitant to ask any questions.

Anne is young; 30 at most. She is a genius, a member of Mensa, the child of two multi-Ph.D.'s. Her background is fascinating. She has been a law enforcement officer, a college teacher and a gifted academic researcher. She is brilliant in the disciplines of math, calculus and applied statistics. She is a true computer wizard—which was the basis of the job she lost yesterday.

What happened? I wish I knew something that would justify the action that management has taken. What I do know is that Anne is a lot smarter that I am. She was probably smarter than most people in our company. She took her intelligence for granted and didn't hide it. That may have been her error. Perhaps, as she matures in this still predominantly male environment, she will learn to better mask her gifts and "go with the political flow." This is a waste and a symptom of the kind of culture that stifles creativity and innovation and instills fear and mediocrity.

Anne had many friends in the company. She was good with people in general and incredible with her internal customers. She worked long hours, often at home with her computer and modem. Many times I would send an electronic message from my machine late in the evening and receive an immediate response.

I'm sure her friends will be disturbed. Worse than that, they will be nervous and cautious. Some will be paranoid just because they knew her and talked with her.

Dr. W. Edwards Deming says:

> What are people afraid of? Afraid to contribute to the company. Better not get out of line. Don't violate procedures. Do it exactly this way.
>
> Why don't they complain to manufacturing about stuff that comes in already defective, hard to work with? No matter what you do, you can't turn out quality work—not within the time allowed. Why don't they say something about that?
>
> Look. Complain to the foreman about it, he can do nothing. Totally helpless about it. You only advance yourself on his list towards the top. And if he has to do some cutting, he begins at the top. Gets rid of the nuisance makers. Asking too many questions that he can't answer will only embarrass him. People don't complain. They don't complain. They have jobs.

Fear takes a horrible toll. Fear is all around, robbing people of their pride, hurting them, robbing them of a chance to contribute to the company. It is unbelievable what happens when you unloose fear.[1]

Given the little I know about Anne, her talent and her willingness to try to improve things, express ideas, make suggestions, talk to her customers, teach others what she knew, I suspect she just went to the top of the list. So, the company lost. Somebody else feels smug, probably, because the nuisance is gone.

I went to lunch with a colleague today. We weren't even to the car before he asked if I had heard that Anne was fired. "Why?" I asked. "Sometimes," he said, "visionaries get squashed."

---

[1] Mary Walton, *The Deming Management Method* (New York: Dodd, Mead & Co., 1986) p. 73.

FIVE . . .

LUNATICS AND

PORCELAIN KNOBS

I really like lunatics. I like being around people who are all fired up about something. It's invigorating. The energy is contagious.

It seems to me that the workplace would be a much greater place to work in if there were a whole bunch more lunatics. From now on, I for one, am only going to hire people with a "high lunatic potential": *HLP*. The reason that seems to make fundamental good sense to me is that when people are lunatics about their work, they'll constantly strive to do their work better.

If leaders are lunatics about the "leader-stuff" they are hired to do, they will discover that one of their jobs is to light the fire under everybody they can so that pretty soon there's a whole room full of lunatics.

I noticed the porcelain knob on one of my kitchen cabinets last night. I thought, yep, there's my knob—right there on my cabinet door. Somewhere, some people are in charge of some kind of process that makes those knobs. If I ran that business, I would want the women and men in charge of those white knobs to be lunatics about white knobs. I would want those men and women to *just love making those knobs*. I would want them to be proud of every single knob they made and to do all they know to make great knobs. I wouldn't tell them how many knobs they had to make or how fast they had to make them. I wouldn't have to do that.

I would just tell them how happy I am that they are going to work in my business and that I want them to make great white knobs. I'd also tell them to let me know if they think of any new kinds of knobs to make. I'd introduce them to everyone else in the company. I'd make sure they had what they needed, and then I would get out of their way.

I like lunatics. I don't like robots. I have trouble understanding and being around unenthusiastic people. I quickly lose interest in people who plow mindlessly through work doing just what they need to do to get by. People turn into robots very quickly if they don't have the freedom to love and enjoy their piece of the work. People shut down their minds and spirits when they aren't having fun doing whatever they are doing. It's a simple fact that people leave places if they aren't having fun. I believe that leaders need to understand and accept that simple fact. I know managers who become suspicious about "production" if they sense that people are happy and having fun. I think that's weird.

In a few days, I get to talk to my boss and his management team. I asked for an an hour on the end of their bi-weekly management team meeting agenda. I want to talk to them about leadership and what Dr. Deming refers to as "joy in work." The people in that room—there will be eight or nine of them—have a profound effect on how 800 people feel everyday. They are the leaders of their organization and what they pay attention to and reinforce is what happens in the organization—whether it's good or not so good.

I'm going to tell them what an executive of Eastman Kodak told me a couple of weeks ago. "Every organization is perfectly designed to get the results it gets." I think there is already one quiet lunatic in that group. This will be my last crack at lighting a few more of them. I don't know if I can do that or not. What I do know is, lighting lunatics is my job—and I love it.

Work takes up so much of our time ... our lives.
It ought to be satisfying and a joy.

NEW TO THE JOB

Katherine was new to the job.

The interview process had been scary. She had mostly told the truth, but she had stretched the depth of her experience just a bit. Anyway, she did a good job with the interview guy. She appeared calm, polished, confident, and knowledgeable. She got the offer. She smiled at the telephone when she accepted the offer. Then, she went out and bought that new suit she had seen in her favorite department store!

So now, it's the first morning, and she's sitting in the chair behind that desk—in the office she had always dreamed about having. She thought, "What the hell do I do now?"

What Katherine decided to do, worked. She got up out of that dreamed-of-chair and left her office and walked around the other office areas. She talked to the people she was about to begin working with. She and the people were nervous, and the moments were awkward at best. Everyone was very polite. People called her Ms. "Last

Name," and she said "Oh no, please, call me 'first name,'" and they all laughed—politically.

She told each of them to make an appointment with her. She told them that she would leave her calendar out on a table in the common area, and they should just write themselves into it where there was a time they liked. They all did—because she was the new boss.

Her meetings with the people started. They went wonderfully because she listened, and she urged them to really talk about what they knew and how they felt. She took notes, and she learned incredible things about the work and the people.

She studied the notes. She did some research. But most important, she went back to each person and discussed the notes and the research and the discoveries. She asked each of them to help her decide what they should do next.

It all worked. She quickly gained the respect and the trust of these new people she was going to work with. She didn't pretend to know important things that they didn't know. She used her judgement and invited each person to blend in theirs, and they shared new discoveries and made great decisions—together. The work improved.

Katherine got the job because of the way she thought about things and because of what she knew about that kind of work. The thing that made her a little different was her willingness to underplay what she knew already, and her wisdom to figure out how to blend her ideas with the ideas of other people who knew things about the work —the work that they all liked to do.

Think of the person you want to talk to.
What would relax them and you?
What do you want to happen? How can you get there?

THE INSPECTOR

AND

THE PROFESSOR

Hank is a meat inspector for the State of Wisconsin: a 25-year veteran of the program. He is good at his job and knows the meat inspection program inside and out—from the guidelines for fat content in hamburger to the regulations for proper cooling of carcasses. Hank had been involved in several team efforts using Quality Improvement methods for six months. He had become a great believer and initiator and motivator in the effort.

On a vacation to Arizona, he visited his daughter Karen, who was going to school at a small, liberal arts college. One evening during his visit, a favorite professor came to visit Karen and meet her parents. Her name was Margaret. She was a sophisticated woman, about 60 years old, with a refined, articulate English accent, and a warm and wonderful manner. She had taught at Oxford University for 30 years and was now teaching in Arizona, including a class in creative writing which Karen was taking.

In their conversation, Margaret began to tell of problems she was having with the class. She was disturbed by the lack of respect students were showing for each other. Students would arrive late or not at all. They would get up and move around the room in the middle of a discussion. They would criticize each other's writing harshly, tearing it apart without respect for the writer's feelings. Their only assignment was to write "something," but they would often come with nothing done.

The whole atmosphere was very upsetting to Margaret. She was from an environment where people demonstrated more respect and courtesy for each other and their work. She didn't know what to do to change things. The school is noted for having a nonstructured philosophy and atmosphere. Classes were supposed to be conducted in a free and open manner. So she felt she could not clamp down on the behavior and set rules. Yet, the atmosphere of the classroom was destructive to creativity and effective learning. She was at a loss as to how to address the problem.

Hank listened to Margaret for a long time, and then he got charged up. Impulsively, he began offering advice. He told her she was right—that the class needed some guidelines for behavior, some ground rules, and some shared goals. But he also said that the students should decide these things for themselves, as a team.

He advised her to get them together, as a team, and guide them in setting those ground rules and goals. He "talked her through" methods for doing so. And he told her they should have "check-ins" and "check-outs"—allowing each person individual time and attention to say what was on their mind at the beginning of class, and then at the end, their evaluation of the class and how they felt.

After the professor left, Hank stopped to realize how impetuous he must have sounded, offering advice to an Oxford professor of 30 years. He feared he had sounded out of line.

A few days later, his daughter called. Margaret had taken Hank's advice and led the class through the steps Hank had recommended, almost word for word. The students set their own ground rules for producing work, being on time, and criticizing work with respect and courtesy for the author's feelings.

And it worked! The same principles that had helped the veteran meat inspectors work together as a team were now helping a class of 18-year-old liberal arts students do the same.

WHEN IT HUMS

When you first get started in Quality Improvement, the skeptics have lots of fuel for fire. There's a big investment of time and money up front. Results take time. Many of the results are "soft," especially when you measure them against hard dollars for training and consulting. But I had a small experience that put it in perspective for me.

Five experienced facilitators were pulled together to make a panel presentation to a group of trainees in Quality Improvement. I was one of them. We were from five different state agencies and we didn't know one another. We met to plan our panel presentation. The meeting was as smooth and productive as any I had ever been to. We found we shared a common knowledge, understanding, and an appreciation for the tools and methods which bring about effective teamwork. In two hours, we got to know each other, felt comfortable, brainstormed tons of ideas, challenged them, sorted them into an order, developed a plan, and had fun doing it.

With that meeting as the only preparation, we delivered the presentation on three afternoons. We worked together like a well-tuned team, passing ideas, supporting each other and building on each other's ideas. The comments from the trainees were excellent including "the best panel presentation I've ever heard." At the end of the three days, we wanted to stay together as a team; we had grown to like and appreciate each other.

The methods and tools of Quality Improvement helped us do this in several ways:

* We used tools that made our decisions and our meeting more effective.

* We were familiar with effective methods for organizing and delivering information.

* We knew how to use constructive conflict; we challenged each other's ideas instead of each other.

* We knew how teamwork and building on each other's ideas would net a better product, so we worked together instead of competing.

* We knew it was okay to have fun. In fact, it enhances creativity. So we had fun.

The most important net result was the effectiveness of the product with a minimum investment. That's what happens when Quality is part of the environment. Once you have it built into the way you operate on a daily basis, things can just hum. When you have that kind of teamwork, with comfortable and satisfied workers—Quality results.

It takes leaders with vision to see beyond the cost/benefit analysis assessment of Quality. Because Quality is not like a form that you use every six months to evaluate workers and set goals.

It is a way of thinking, acting, working, and doing business—every day.

HOW TO GIVE
THIS BOOK
TO YOUR BOSS

Many people who have read this book have responded by wanting to give it to their bosses. Following are some suggestions for various ways to give this book to your boss.

The straight-forward approach:

"Good morning, Boss. I just finished reading this book and I think it is worth reading. I thought you might also enjoy it. Would you care to borrow my copy?"

The butter-up approach:

"Hello, Boss. I loved the way you_____
the other day. It is an example of your great
leadership style. I was also reminded of your style
and methods as I read a new book about leadership,
Real People, Real Work. I think you would enjoy
it. Would you like to borrow my copy?"

The pressure approach:

(*This is done in front of an audience of staff or peers. It
works best if the person's boss is making the presentation.*)

"This book is being presented to Ms. Jones in
recognition of her efforts to continually grow, as
demonstrated by the accomplishments she has
made over the last few years. It is a book about
leadership in the 90's, and we know that Ms. Jones
will be right out there, in the forefront, learning
and continuing to grow."

The anonymous approach, sent in fear:

(This message is done with cut-out letters from newspapers and magazines, pasted on a piece of notebook paper. The book is enclosed. It is placed on the boss' desk in the night.)

> "Read this and you will learn the real reason people skip out of work, customers are going to our competitors, and our widgets fall apart."

If you are a boss ...
watch for these subtle messages.

DISCUSSION STARTERS . . .

STORIES BY
KEY TOPICS

We hope these stories or parables bring depth to your thoughts on leadership. We hesitate, for that reason, to categorize the stories by "key topics." However, you may find this useful to help focus training and discussions on the stories.

LEADERSHIP

All the stories illustrate principles of leadership.

CUSTOMER FOCUS

DISCUSSION STARTERS

INVISIBLE STAR and FIVE STAR ASSOCIATE

(These two stories (on pages 11 and 15) can be used together. Read both, then compare them.)

Key Topics: customer focus, worker perspective, trust and fear, all one team, joy in work

Compare the golf club and the hotel environments of Helen and Gayle.

How does the environment effect their performance and job satisfaction?

How does it affect the Customers and the success of the business?

Who wins in each story and who loses?

How do the employees in your organization feel about their jobs? How do you know? How can you find out?

PANTYHOSE—RUNS IN THE CHARTS
(Page 17)

Key Topics: customer focus, process and data

Did the executives of this organization know what was important to their customers? Did they think they knew?

How were they measuring success? How should they be measuring success?

What are the measures of success of your organization? How do you measure it?

How can you learn what your customers think of your products and services?

As a customer, what can you do to let your suppliers know what you think of their products? When and why should you do this?

THE GUY IN THE BOX IN THE LOBBY
(Page 23)

Key Topics: customer focus, all one team, worker perspective

What are the first contacts you have with your organization? Who is in those jobs? What information and tools do they need?

Think about first contacts you have had with organizations, in person, on the phone, or through the mail. What impressions did you get? What gave you those impressions?

If you were the guy in the box, what could you do to try to improve your work situation?

Where are there "guys in boxes" in your organization?

How can you find out what people need to do their jobs?

How can you make people in your organization feel safe to say what they need to do their jobs?

How can you help people be aware of what they might need to do their jobs? What might help them improve the work they do or the services they provide?

OWNING THE FIX
(Page 31)

Key Topics: **all one team, worker perspective, process and data**

Do you think Sharon's and Carla's contributions enhanced the results of this situation? How?

How would this level of duplication exist without being recognized? Could this exist in your organization? How can you work to identify those that exist and avoid future ones developing?

What do you think Sharon and Carla learned from this experience? What did the analysts learn? What did the organization and customers gain?

What do you think would have happened if the analyst had conducted the study themselves and come up with the same recommendation? How is this like the role of auditors and other program reviewers?

Are there responsibilities that people have in your organization that set up win-lose situations? How might this be improved?

COACHING SOCCER
(Page 43)

Key Topics: process and data, all one team

This story is about soccer. What else might these principles and methods apply to? How?

Talk about variation. What does it mean? Where does it exist in your work?

How does variation effect results in your processes?

What errors can be made in decisions if variation is not understood?

Where does it seem that staff may not be "trying hard"? Might there be process improvements that could help them to do their best work?

TAKE OFF YOUR COAT AND HAVE A SEAT
(Page 47)

Key Topics: process and data, all one team

What are major problems in your work area right now?

What is being done to fix them?

What is being done to learn the root causes?

Are the people who do the work being involved in the improvement process?

Are the customers involved?

INVOLVE ME, I'LL UNDERSTAND
(Page 51)

**Key Topics: all one team, worker perspective,
process and data**

Why did the workers accept the recommendation after the work sessions? How much of the whole situation do you think they understood before the work sessions?

Remember the nursery rhyme with the many blind men touching the elephant and "seeing" the elephant differently? Relate that story to this.

Think about the disagreements about changes that are currently going on in your work place. Think about who is upset and why. Do you think they understand the whole picture? How can you help them see a broader view?

SARA—DOING THE WRONG STUFF RIGHT
(Page 57)

Key Topics: **customer focus (internal), process and data, worker perspective**

Who was Sara's customer? Did she know what her customer needed? Did she think she knew? (Compare Sara with the pantyhose company for this question—internal and external customers.)

Do you think Sara has a view of the organization beyond her individual tasks? How would it help her to have a broader view? How can she get it?

Imagine you are Sara's supervisor and just had this conversation with her. What would you do now? What would you say to Sara and how would you say it?

What might you do to find out if other similar non-work activities exist in your work area? What can you do to ensure that new non-work activities don't develop?

DEAR BOSS
(Page 63)

Key Topics: trust and fear

Have you ever felt fear in your job? What factors contributed to that?

What toll does fear take? What are the effects and impacts? How does fear affect job performance?

Do you see signs of fear in your work place? What are the "undiscussable" subjects in your work area?

Relate this story to "Anne Shire Got Fired" (page 97).

Do you think that some factors which contribute to fear are intentional? Or are they due to a lack of understanding of their impact?

How can the organization and supervisors become more aware of the signs of fear and contributing factors?

UNCHAINED MELANY
(Page 75)

Key Topics: worker perspective, joy in work

What did Melany need in order to be able to do her best work?

Why didn't previous managers provide what she needed?

Discuss John's role and style as her manager.

WORKING HARD AND FALLING BEHIND
(Page 95)

Key Topics: process and data

Is there a process that seems complex in your area?

List *only* the steps that are needed when there are *no* exceptions or problems.

Now list all the steps, including decision points, delays, and loops back.

These extra steps are "complexity." How can you get rid of them?

NEW TO THE JOB
(Page 107)

Key Topics: Trust and Fear

Discuss Katherine's actions as a new manager.

Talk about the perspective of her staff.

Compare other ways of getting started.

Compare this story to "Unchained Melany" (page 75). Compare it with "Dear Boss" (page 63).

WHEN IT HUMS
(Page 117)

Key Topics: joy in work, all one team

Talk about work experiences when things "hummed."

What were the elements that contributed to the success?

How might you work to build in those factors into other work situations?

TELL YOUR OWN STORY

The stories in *Real People, Real Work* are simple examples of things that happen around all of us daily. Look around you. Think about the everyday interactions you have. Think about the frustrating moments. Think about the times when things really click and hum. Think about the big "aha's" that smack you in the face with simple wisdom.

Write or outline them, or tell them. Or act them out. Then guide a discussion. The following questions may help you.

* What work is being done in this story?
  What is the value or mission? For whom?
  To accomplish what?

* Who are the customers? What is important
  to them? How can their needs be better met?

* What is the role and value of the workers?
  The leaders? What could be done to streng-
  then contributions of each?

* What is the process? What data and facts are
  being used to make decisions? What should
  or could be used to enhance this?

ABOUT THE AUTHORS

Lee Cheaney is a private consultant working with companies nationwide. He has served as the Director of Quality Leadership for Epson America, Inc. in Torrance, California, and he was a prime initiator and developer of Quality leadership methods in state government in Wisconsin. He was a prime mover in the development of a major Quality network in Wisconsin, linking public and private organizations, and is now doing the same in the South Bay area of California. He has gained an international reputation as a motivational speaker, using real people in his talks, as in these stories. Lee has a Bachelor of Arts degree in Sociology and Psychology from the University of Colorado and an MPA in Finance from Indiana University.

Maury Cotter is a Management Consultant in the Office of Quality at the University of Wisconsin, Madison campus. There, she helped initiate and develop their implementation efforts. She has worked as the Quality Coordinator for a Wisconsin state agency where she helped initiate and develop a comprehensive effort. She has been a leader in the development of consortiums of public sector agencies to develop Quality training. She has worked with numerous public and private sector agencies over the last 17 years as a consultant, facilitator, and speaker. She has a BA degree in English from the University of Wisconsin, Madison. Cotter lives in Madison with her husband, John, and children, Kelly and Adam.

Lee and **Maury** give individual and joint programs focused on linking the principles and methods of Quality to real people and real work. The presentations are lively, woven throughout with dozens of stories which drive home the points. In their presentations, Lee and Maury interact, role play, and involve the audience in connecting the stories to the theories.

147